# SHIPS

Library of Congress Cataloging-in-Publication Data:
Plisson, Philip.
Ships / Philip Plisson.
p. cm.
ISBN-13: 978-0-8109-1624-1 (hardcover with jkt.)
ISBN-10: 0-8109-1624-X (hardcover with jkt.)
1. Ships—Juvenile literature.  I. Title.
VM150.P585 2007
623.82—DC22
2006039337

All photographs by Philip Plisson except:
pages 16–17: copyright © Guillaume Plisson
page 27: copyright © Didier Perron

Copyright © 2007 Éditions de la Martinière, Paris
Translated by Christopher Pitts
English translation copyright © 2007 Abrams Books for Young Readers, New York

Printed and bound in Belgium
10 9 8 7 6 5 4 3 2 1

**HNA**
harry n. abrams, inc.
a subsidiary of La Martinière Groupe
115 West 18th Street
New York, NY 10011
www.hnabooks.com

# PHILIP PLISSON ⚓

# SHIPS

Text by Anne Jankeliowitch

Illustrations by John Pendray ⚓
official painter of the French navy

ABRAMS BOOKS FOR YOUNG READERS

NEW YORK

# CONTENTS

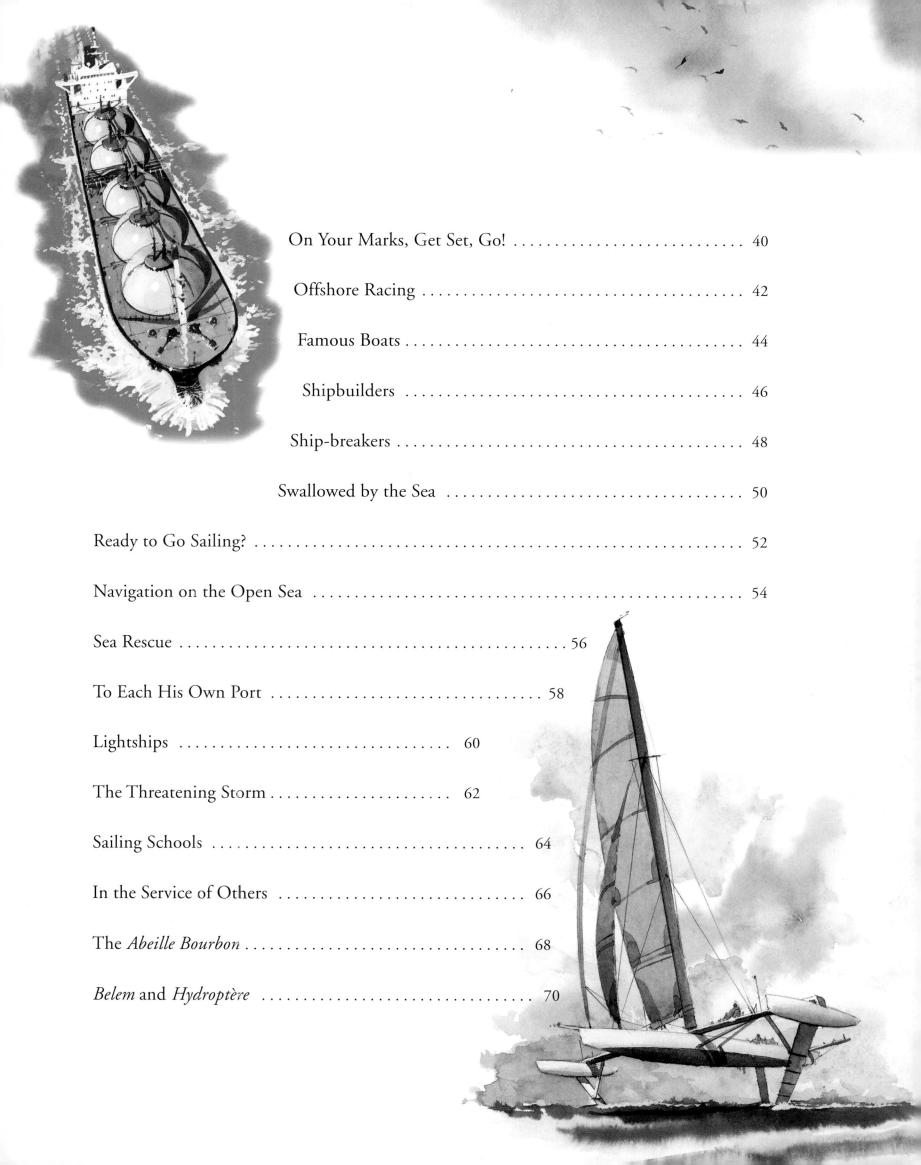

# Those who love the sea love the waves, the smell of salt air, the coastlines, the sailors, the lighthouses, and of course, the ships.

All of those ships . . . Philip knows quite a lot about them. He has photographed the planet's oceans for more than thirty years, and traveled through more than fifty countries. His passport contains a complete set of international visas! And, over the course of his travels, he has encountered a wide variety of ships, in various shapes and sizes, which are used for all sorts of different purposes. He has photographed them from helicopters, other boats, and even while on board with the crew. He has traveled through the frozen Baltic Sea on an icebreaker, sailed around Cape Horn with the *Jeanne d'Arc*, crossed the English Channel in the bridge of a ferry, dived to the depths in a nuclear submarine, toured Venice in a gondola, swam in the pool of a luxury yacht, and crossed the Atlantic on a sailing boat. When he isn't out at sea, he travels to the great shipyards of the world, where ocean liners and enormous freighters are built, or attends tall-ship gatherings and regattas, or even searches for spectacular shipwrecks.

The seas that surround Philip's native country, France—the Mediterranean, the Atlantic, the English Channel, and the North Sea—make for
a rich variety of landscapes and stories, and are an integral part of the work
and life of people and their ships.

But in spite of its importance, the ocean, like its ships, is
often neglected and even forgotten by many classes in
school. It is barely covered in geography textbooks and
atlases; nor is it given much importance in higher educa-
tion. And yet, on Earth, the oceans occupy considerably
more space than the continents. They contain a vital
food supply for humanity, and it is through their waters
that most of the world's trade is conducted. You might even
wonder if planet Earth shouldn't be called planet Ocean!
Without going quite that far, we hope that this book will,
to some extent, shed light on this neglected topic and
bring inspiration to young sailors everywhere.

# Every Ship Reflects Humanity in Its Own Way . .

Sails to the wind, an old sailing ship glides elegantly across a calm sea. Its shadow, slender and majestic, inspires a daydream. Imagine being on board, in far-off seas, in another time . . . All ships carry the promise of adventure.

Since the dawn of time, people have dreamed of exploring the seas. The first ships, built during the Stone Age, were most likely simple log rafts. Over the course of tens of thousands of years, inventions have transformed them: First oars were added, then sails, and, finally, engines. For millennia, boats were made of wood; it was only in the twentieth century that steel took its place for building commercial and military vessels, while plastic transformed pleasure boats. The Egyptians, Vikings, Chinese, Spanish, and Portuguese have all traveled the seas for centuries, and their longships, galleons, and caravels continue to sail today through the pages of history books. The sea remains an important means of transportation and gathering food, as well as a source of enjoyment for all those who have ever stepped on board a pleasure boat or a luxury cruise liner. It is also a living museum, with its traditional tall ships participating in gatherings and races throughout the world, and a virtual history book, with its multiple shipwrecks that tell of different eras.

Ships tell the story of progress. Ferdinand Magellan was the first man to circumnavigate the world by sea. He left Europe in 1519 with five vessels and 265 men, taking three years to complete his voyage. Only one ship returned, with just eighteen men on board—but the first circumnavigation of the world had been achieved. Today, yachtsmen with racing boats participate in the Jules Verne Trophy, sailing a similar route in just fifty days!

Whether it is traditional, modern, local, or foreign, every ship is a descendant of the world's first boat, and tells the story of humankind in its own unique way.

A small Turkish freighter loaded with fuel battles a storm.

# The History of Ships

In the nineteenth century, clippers were used to transport goods. They left Europe with coal or manufactured products that were traded for cotton, tea, or spices in Asia and coffee in Central and South America.

About ten thousand years ago, people discovered that by hollowing out a tree trunk with stone tools, they could travel on water. This invention was the first step in the history of ships. Since then, boats have continued to evolve to serve the needs of transportation, fishing, exploration, trade, and warfare.

The great maritime discoveries began over three thousand years ago. The Maoris ventured out on enormous two-hulled dugouts that were capable of carrying up to fifty people, together with domestic animals and supplies, for several months. In this way, they populated the Pacific islands—and all this happened more than 2,500 years before Christopher Columbus landed in the New World! In the Middle Ages, the Vikings crossed the Atlantic with their *drakkars* (longships), and in the fifteenth century, the Chinese official Zheng He sailed, it is said, with a fleet of seventy junks, the largest of which had nine masts.

Later, ships became more specialized. One type of ship was the fishing vessel, which has evolved into today's factory ship. Another type of ship was used for military navies. In the eighteenth century, military vessels were equipped with up to seventy-four canons and eight hundred sailors. Today, we have aircraft carriers and nuclear submarines. A third type of ship was used for trade, like the famous three- or four-mast clippers eventually replaced at the beginning of the twentieth century by steam-powered vessels, which traveled faster. Today, a vast array of freighters transport all sorts of merchandise around the world. The final category of ships is pleasure boats. They are powered by either the wind or an engine, and are used for cruises and racing.

**This model boat found in the tomb of Tutankhamen (King Tut) dates to 1346 B.C.E.**

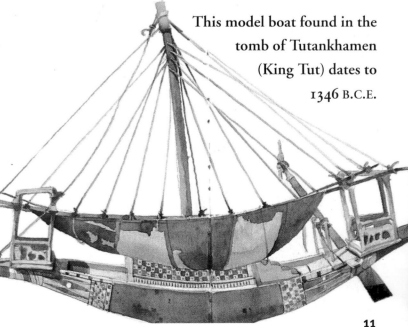

# Monohulls

Designed by the famous naval architect William Fife, *Mariquita*, christened in 1911, quickly made a name for itself as a formidable competitor in regattas. Completely restored, this 115-foot sailing boat, soon to be one hundred years of age, is today one of the most beautiful and fastest cruising yachts on the seas.

All monohull sailing boats have, as their name indicates, a single hull. Another thing they have in common is what is called "listing," which means that the force of the wind filling the sails causes the boat to lean to one side. So why don't they capsize? Their hulls contain lead or iron ballast, which acts as a counterweight to maintain stability. And how is it that boats can sail against the wind, which is known as sailing "close-hauled"? To do so, they have to move diagonally like a crab, catching the wind as it blows from the side. The secret to sailing upwind is also found beneath the hull. The keel, which is rigid and heavy (it holds the ballast), holds the boat on course and keeps it from drifting. On dinghies (as opposed to keeled boats), the keel is replaced by a centerboard that can be taken out of the water; the ballast is located inside the hull. On smaller sport boats, there is no ballast at all: The crewmembers act as a counterweight by "trapezing." They hang off the side of the boat by attaching themselves with a line and pushing onto the hull with their feet. On larger racing boats, you will sometimes see the entire crew sitting on the same side of the boat with their legs dangling in the air so as to increase the counterweight, which limits the listing of the boat. If a sailing boat lists too much, the sails are not as high and thus they catch less wind, which slows the boat down. This won't help you win any regattas!

When you are unaccustomed to listing, it can be surprising. However, it is a fundamental aspect of sailing, and boats are designed with listing in mind. Motorized monohulls do not list.

**Elegant mahogany steamboats were used for river travel at the turn of the twentieth century.**

13

# Multihulls

*Fujicolor* is part of the giant trimaran family. Only used for open-sea racing, these powerful and sophisticated sailing boats with a width of more than sixty feet and a hundred-foot mast can reach a speed of more than twenty-one miles per hour. But watch out it doesn't break!

The velocity of a boat is slowed by the resistance of the water. To reduce this resistance, or "wave drag," and thus increase the boat's speed, as little of the hull as possible should be in contact with the water. This is the main principle behind multihulls, which have several narrow hulls instead of one large hull, as with the monohulls.

Enough spacing between the hulls results in a boat that is particularly stable. This means that sailing boats can use even larger sails, which allows them to go faster. Multihull sailing boats require delicate handling. The catamaran has two identical hulls joined by crossbeams with a net (the trampoline) in between them. The proa, originally from Malaysia and Indonesia, has a main hull and a smaller, parallel hull (known as an outrigger) to provide balance; the latter must always face the wind. Three hulls make up a trimaran, which has one main hull flanked by two outrigger hulls. The windward hull (the side of the boat facing the wind) is lifted out of the water, which helps the boat to go even faster.

The catamaran is also used for pleasure sailing: Stable, spacious, and without a keel (which allows it to go into very shallow areas), it has a number of strong points. There is also a motorized form used for passenger transport: Express ferries are often catamarans.

Of course, you cannot increase the number of hulls forever. And yet . . . pentamarans (five hulls used for heavy loads) are currently being designed for future shipping boats!

**Catamarans are gaining popularity as express ferries, like this one on the San Francisco Bay.**

# Boats with Oars and Paddles

Four different ways of rowing (clockwise from top left): energetically for the members of a whitewater rafting crew, perseveringly for the ocean-crossing *Aude Fontenoy*, artfully for Eric Tabarly sculling in the harbor of La Trinité-sur-Mer, and serenely for Ernestine on the *Marie Galante*.

I n ancient times, ships were powered by slaves who were forced to row until they were overcome with exhaustion. Viking *drakkars* (longships) used oars as well as sails. Today, we row for pleasure and sport. Competitive rowing, which began in the eighteenth century, consists of racing a boat (the skiff) using long oars. Skiffs are long and narrow in order to reduce water resistance and improve glide. For example, an eight-person skiff is about sixty feet long, but only twenty-two inches wide.

Rowing also allows you to move a small craft short distances, thus avoiding the need to equip a boat with a motor. But if you want, you can also cross the Atlantic or Pacific by yourself in a rowing boat. You just need lots of free time!

Unlike an oar, a paddle is not attached to a boat. A canoe, a dugout canoe, or a raft (a large inflatable boat used for navigating rivers) is maneuvered by means of a single paddle, while the kayak uses a double paddle.

The oar family also includes the scull, a single oar placed behind a boat that serves both to propel and steer the vessel. The technique, which consists of tracing a figure eight in the water, requires much skill. If you ever see someone nonchalantly using a scull with one hand while seemingly thinking of other things, that person has undoubtedly had many hours of practice.

Today, the hulls of these boats are made of carbon fiber or fiberglass. However, this one is made of laminated wood.

# Motorboats

With its V-shaped stem designed to cut through the waves, the 118 WallyPower can travel at a speed of sixty-eight miles per hour, even in rough seas. Its metallic hull conceals a luxurious and spacious interior.

Today's engine and propeller are the descendants of the eighteenth-century steam engine. Coal was the most common fuel used to create steam, which was then harnessed to turn the gears. Today, smaller boats are powered by outboard motors (attached to the exterior of the hull at the stern of the boat) that run on gas, while larger engines run on diesel. Some ships use nuclear energy. This is the case with many submarines (because atomic propulsion does not require air) and some icebreakers, which can then sail through frozen seas for several years.

Large freighters, designed for transporting heavy cargo loads, are equipped with the largest diesel engines in the world, and their engine rooms are supervised from separate control centers. The mechanic is isolated from the heat and constant drone and is surrounded by buttons, screens, and all sorts of controls, like on a flight deck.

Engines are also used for pleasure boating. In fact, they are more or less required; many of the pleasure boats in the United Kingdom are motorboats. But motorized luxury yachts, like those of the 118 WallyPower series—with a length of 118 feet and three 5,600-horsepower turbines that propel it at a speed of sixty knots (seventy miles per hour) and the intriguing allure of a stealth frigate—are toys only a very few can afford.

This small coal-burning steam coaster from the 1920s is used as a supply ship for the Scottish isles.

# How Are New Ships Built?

In the eighteenth century, the shipyards at Brest, Toulon, and Rochefort provided vessels for the French navy. The hull of a seventy-four-canon ship required around 2,800 hundred-year-old oak trees and nearly one year of work. The frigate *Hermione*, a 145-foot-long three-master, here in construction at Rochefort, is a replica of the original, which sailed in 1780.

If you want to design a new boat, you need to hire a naval architect. The future owner (or, if it is a commercial boat, the company that will use it) will specify the main criteria, identifying all the important characteristics of the boat. For example, the owner may want to transport a certain number of tons of a certain amount of ore (a freighter) or a certain number of passengers (a ferry), or have a ship that is spacious and elegant (a yacht) or fast and easy to handle (a racing boat). Of course, boats must also meet other criteria: They have to be stable, strong, safe, and inexpensive. After determining the specifications, the architect need only take up the challenge and begin working on the designs.

First sketches give an idea as to the dimensions, the volume, the shape of the submerged part of the hull, and the silhouette of the craft as a whole. The architect then draws up the exact blueprints for each part of the ship, from the keel to the cabins. For the ocean liner RMS *Queen Mary 2*, there were more than ten thousand blueprints. For a passenger ship, it is also necessary to provide an evacuation plan in case of a shipwreck. It is hoped, of course, that it will never have to be used.

Naval architects used to draw up all their blueprints by hand on large sheets of paper. But modern naval architecture makes use of software. Everything is done on a computer, and the various calculations that help determine the shape of the hull are carried out by specialized programs. Then the architect makes a small model that is tested in a special wave pool to evaluate the performance of the design in different currents and conditions. It is also possible to do testing by means of digital simulation, but it's not nearly as much fun!

# Sailing Boats

In 1992 in San Diego, California, the America's Cup was sailed for the first time with yachts belonging to the International America's Cup Class. Handled by top crews and assisted by computers, these sophisticated boats are true racing machines.

Where do you find a topsail, a forestaysail, a flying jib, a topgallant sail, and a royal sail? On the mast! In the time of the great sailing ships, which lasted until the nineteenth century, every sail on the great galleons that traveled the seas had its own name, and there were dozens of them. The bigger the ship, the more sails it needed for propulsion. In order for sails to remain small enough so that sailors could still handle them, masts were lengthened and the number of sails on each mast was increased. Ships with as many as six or seven masts were built. The sails, made out of thick, strong cotton cloth, were extremely heavy and difficult to hoist. A small army of topmen (sailors) would bustle about working with the ropes, sometimes at a great height above the sea. It was a dangerous task, because a fall meant certain death, as ships couldn't turn around to rescue a man who fell overboard.

Most modern sailing ships are used only for pleasure or racing. The shapes of sails have since evolved to become more efficient. Today, the Marconi rig, with triangular sails that can be maneuvered quickly and easily, is the most common. Can you find the spinnaker? This large colored sail is used when the wind blows from behind, while the storm jib, a small sail in the fore, is used to stabilize the boat and keep it maneuverable during large gusts of wind. Thanks to synthetic fibers, sails are now lighter, more rigid, and more durable. Racing boats use Kevlar for their enormous rigging, and crewmembers can move sails as large as basketball courts effortlessly and safely.

Old ships required many sails.

# Fishing Boats

On a fishing boat, the incessant rolling, the omnipresent salt water, and the exhausting physical demands on fishermen make voyages at sea as grueling as they are dangerous.

Anyone who has ever done any fishing knows the joy of reeling in a catch! But for some people, fishing is a job. And it's one of the most dangerous ones there is, with exhausting living and working conditions and the constant threat of danger.

Catching each species of fish requires its own technique. Tuna and anchovies, for example, swim in schools (groups of fish), and are caught with large nets dragged behind boats called trawlers. Scallops and shrimp, which live in the sea bottom, are gathered with a dredge (a large net that scrapes the ocean floor), while lobster are caught in traps. The name of the type of boat often indicates the catch: There are tuna boats, sardine boats, shrimp boats, and in the past, even whale boats.

Traditional fishing is done by day, along the coast. Often, birds help to locate the fish. Flocks congregate above the schools on which they feed. In contrast, industrial trawlers may go to sea for months on end. Schools are located using sonar (an instrument that uses sound waves to locate objects underwater), or even from airplanes. Once fish are caught, they are then sorted, cleaned, and frozen or canned on board the ship. These factory ships are capable of catching one hundred tons of fish per hour—about as much as a sixteenth-century fishing boat would catch in an entire season! The result? People are catching fish at a rate that is much too high. Schools of fish are becoming increasingly smaller, and, without time to replenish themselves, they are slowly dwindling in number. One day, there won't be enough fish left to catch. Will we be able to reach a balance before it is too late?

**An Icelandic trawler weathers choppy waters in the North Atlantic.**

# Ships from Around the World

*Jangadas* are traditional sailing boats used for fishing in the northeast of Brazil. There are about twenty thousand remaining along the coast. Simple and rudimentary, they nevertheless fearlessly travel hundreds of miles along the coast for several days, braving violent storms.

There are as many different styles of ships as there are countries with coastlines. Each culture invented the boat that best served it for fishing or transportation, using the materials at hand and according to the limitations of the local environment.

The Inuit in the Arctic, for example, traditionally built their kayaks out of seal skin. These small, light boats are easily transported over ice when hunting seals. The Indians in the Amazon hollowed out large tree trunks to make long dugout canoes, which allowed them to navigate river channels easily. The Polynesians fished from dugout canoes equipped with outriggers (a lateral support float connected to the hull by two crossbeams). This kept the craft high in the water for navigating lagoons and coral reefs.

In some areas, traditional boats are also used in regattas. The *yoles* from Martinique, simple sailing boats originally used for coastal fishing, are today sailed in popular water-jousting tournaments.

Other boats have become symbolic of their part of the world, like Chinese junks, flat-bottomed ships with rectangular sails tightened by strips of bamboo. The enormous Polynesian outrigger canoes are even included on the country's flag. All these vessels are inseparable from their cultural origins. Imagine, for example, seeing a Venetian gondola on the Thames. Or a skiff amid Brazilian *jangadas* on the Amazon . . .

**This Balinese trimaran has a carved swordfish prow.**

# Ferries and Ocean Liners

A dozen maritime routes, like the one taken by this ship from Brittany Ferries embarking from the port of Caen, connect England with France. Each day, 63,000 passengers are carried on the ferries' 130 crossings from one country to the other.

Ocean liners appeared around 1840, and until the development of commercial air travel (in the 1960s), they were the sole means available for crossing the world's great oceans. Planes, which covered long distances in a shorter amount of time, gradually led to the disappearance of regular maritime routes and put the great ocean liners into retirement.

Today, passenger ships are mainly used for short distances between two nearby coasts (straits, islands, lakes). RORO (roll on/roll off) vessels, used to transport cars and trucks, are more commonly known as ferries. A ferry generally has a large hold for vehicles (which roll on to the ship via a ramp) and separate passenger decks. The largest can carry up to five hundred vehicles on several levels. For passenger transportation, most people prefer express ferries. These are usually catamarans, but there are also hovercrafts (boats that float on a cushion of air and are propelled by aerial propellers).

Ferries are very large ships, and also have a shallow draught (the depth of a ship's hull submerged in water). And there sure is a lot of room inside. However, because of this, these ships are not stable enough to travel on the ocean. That's why you can't cross the Atlantic on a ferry. However, on an ocean liner, you won't have to worry, as long as you have a couple of days free in your schedule. Cruise ships have become so popular that the number of large ocean liners continues to increase to this day.

**American paddleboats transported merchandise and passengers on large rivers such as the Mississippi.**

# Steel Giants Filled with Oil

The supertanker *New Wisdom* is embarking from an oil terminal on the Donge River. It will fill its tanks with crude oil after arriving in the Persian Gulf. The white superstructure rising above the ship's stern and topped by the bridge is called a castle.

NO SMOKING

NEW WISDOM

BRITTA ODE

The oil tanker family includes the world's largest ships. These steel monsters can be as long as 1,500 feet and carry up to 300,000 tons of crude oil (oil that will be transformed through refining into different types of fuel) in their holds. The longest and heaviest ship ever built was the supertanker *Knock Nevis*: It is 1,500 feet long and weighs 650,000 tons when loaded.

Oil tankers are also the world's most dangerous boats, because they carry hydrocarbons that can cause catastrophic oil slicks. They are so dangerous, in fact, they must never be allowed to dock by themselves. The threat of an accident happening is constant, even in port, and it is out of the question to even take the slightest risk. Tugboats are responsible for maneuvering tankers into a port.

Once offshore, accidents are harder to avoid. If oil spills from the ship, it creates a slick that kills thousands of marine animals and pollutes hundreds of miles of coastline. One ton of oil can spread over a surface equivalent to 1,700 football fields. To improve security, oil tankers will be, in principle, built with a double hull beginning in 2015. In this system, a space of approximately six feet will separate the two hulls. In the event of an accident, the oil in the hold (the interior of the hull) will spill in between the two hulls instead of polluting the sea. It is a good idea, but will it be enough to prevent further catastrophes?

**Feluccas and *gailassas* still travel up the Nile in Egypt.**

# Warships

In 2005, to celebrate the bicentennial of the Battle of Trafalgar, an armada of yachts and old sailing vessels escorted more than one hundred battleships for a fleet review in the Solent, the channel between mainland England and the Isle of Wight.

Not so long ago, incredible naval battles took place involving dozens of military ships shooting canons at one another. Navies today consist of a variety of warships, ranging from patrol vessels and aircraft carriers to submarines. The U.S. Navy dates back to the American Revolution and currently has 500,000 personnel on active duty, along with 278 ships. But what's the use of having a fleet of warships in the twenty-first century?

Nuclear submarines serve as an important deterrent. Indeed, they are used to discourage any other country that has the intention of attacking the United States by showing them the types of reprisals they risk. To do this, the submarines traverse the murky depths of the world's oceans, without anyone knowing their exact location.

Other warships land troops for ground combat, launch bomber planes from aircraft carriers, protect supply convoys (for food, medicine, and weapons), or destroy the enemy's supply lines to weaken their position.

In peacetime, Navy boats carry out maritime surveillance and other missions. They help with rescue operations and oil-slick cleanup, and they participate in scientific missions and help update nautical charts. During natural catastrophes or other emergencies, they help evacuate civilians and save lives.

# A Vast Array of Cargo

The giant cargo ship *Otello*, a colossus more than 980 feet long, 130 feet wide, and with a draught of 45 feet, can transport 8,500 containers.

Today, 90 percent of goods traded throughout the world are transported by ship. Merchants have a plethora of freighters at their disposable for specialized cargo. LPG tankers, for example, are equipped with tanks maintained at a temperature of -250°F to keep methane in its liquid state (which is less spacious than its gaseous state). Bulk carriers are loaded with grain, wood, or cement, while chemical tankers have special reinforced tanks for transporting chemical substances.

Container ships are loaded with stacks of giant metal boxes (containers), which are all the same size (twenty feet long) and carry all sorts of manufactured products. The load can be piled as high as twenty stories! To counterbalance the top weight, the base of the hull contains ballast, special compartments filled with water. These are the same containers that you see on trucks and freight trains: Once a container is unloaded from a ship, it continues its journey on land. The system is so simple and practical that it has revolutionized shipping throughout the world.

Thirty years ago, the largest container ship could hold three thousand containers. Today, they carry 9,500, and freighters capable of holding 18,000 containers are already being designed. It seems like nothing can slow down the growth of container ships. Asia (and, in particular, China) has become the new "workshop of the world." It imports raw materials in bulk carriers and exports manufactured products in containers to destinations across the globe, which is consuming more and more. But soon, many ports will no longer be deep enough, nor have the equipment capable of harboring these giants.

This ship carrying liquid gas in its tanks is one of the most complex vessels used in the merchant marine.

# Pleasure Boats

Not far from Cassis, a fishing village on the Mediterranean, a sailing boat prepares to drop anchor. The sunlight is perfect, the surroundings are magical, and the place is deserted. What more could you ask for?

L ife on board a large pleasure boat brings a feeling of escape and freedom. With a pleasure boat, you can drop anchor at magical spots and sail along vast, undeveloped shorelines, far from the crowds.

But in pleasure boating you still have to get from one destination to another. Using the wind for fuel and the sails for a motor, and without creating noise or pollution, fortunate sailors await other moments of bliss.

But, when sailing, you can always encounter bad weather, and sometimes you will even run into storms. You can get seasick, be delayed by a breakdown, or need to repair a broken part. You can get tired of listing (when the wind rolls the boat to one side), of having poorly stored items crashing about, of the humidity and the lack of space, and of the fatigue that comes with being on watch instead of sleeping at night. Even after you have dropped anchor, a gust of wind can always blow up and push the boat dangerously close to the rocks, which means you have to go through the entire anchoring process again . . .

All of these experiences are also a part "pleasure" sailing. So, for amateurs, it's best to remember the drawbacks so that your dream doesn't suddenly turn into a nightmare!

# Golden Faucets

Luxury yachting has become increasingly popular, and private yachts, like this one, are becoming more and more numerous. The largest and most luxurious yacht in the world is the *Project Platinum*, which belongs to the emir of Dubai. It is 525 feet long—half the length of an aircraft carrier.

The taste for luxury on the high seas is by no means recent. At the beginning of the twentieth century, transatlantic liners were already considered to be "floating palaces." The dining hall of the *Normandie*, the French ocean liner christened in 1935, was larger than the Hall of Mirrors at the Palace of Versailles. The ship was also known by the prestigious nickname "the Vessel of Light."

On today's private luxury yachts, you can find everything you've ever dreamed of. On board the *Octopus*, there is a movie theater, a pool, a nightclub, a basketball court, two heliports, and even a submarine. On the deck of another yacht, there is a speedboat, a helicopter, and a forty-foot sailing boat. Maintaining just one of these ships requires sixty crew members and $2 million a month. Polished from morning to night by the sailors, these ships must always be impeccable in the event that their owner should suddenly decide to set sail. In the world of luxury yachting, everything seems possible.

Each year in Monaco, an exclusive yacht show displays one hundred of these dream boats, with half of them more than 130 feet long. Don't bother trying to sneak a peak from the quays; the guests are invited according to the size of their wallets. Some yachts are available for hire. At $400,000 per week, it's a real deal!

# On Your Marks, Get Set, Go!

The starting point of a regatta is an imaginary line that extends from a buoy to the racing committee's boat, equipped with a jackstaff. In principle, the line is perpendicular to the direction of the wind, and the racing committee's boat is, as here, to the right of the boats.

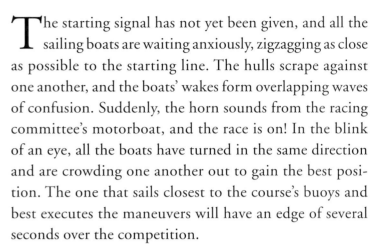

The starting signal has not yet been given, and all the sailing boats are waiting anxiously, zigzagging as close as possible to the starting line. The hulls scrape against one another, and the boats' wakes form overlapping waves of confusion. Suddenly, the horn sounds from the racing committee's motorboat, and the race is on! In the blink of an eye, all the boats have turned in the same direction and are crowding one another out to gain the best position. The one that sails closest to the course's buoys and best executes the maneuvers will have an edge of several seconds over the competition.

In a regatta, the winner is the boat that completes the course marked by buoys in the fastest possible time. It's not enough to know how to handle your boat well: Being clever is often what makes the difference. Some courses are for boats of a specific category, known as a "class" (determined according to the size of the hull and sails). For example, in the America's Cup, boats are on average seventy-two feet long with gigantic sails rigged to a mast more than one hundred feet tall— as tall as a ten-story building. This column is so large that a person can fit inside! Since its beginning in 1851, the America's Cup has continued to fascinate the public. It is the world's most watched sporting event after the Olympic Games and the World Cup.

When a regatta takes place on the open seas as opposed to on a harbor or lake, it is known as an offshore race, like the transatlantic Route du Rhum. The greatest race of all consists of sailing across the world's oceans to circumnavigate the globe.

# Offshore Racing

Speedboat races take place on the ocean and also on lakes, where the calm waters allow the boats to perform exceptionally. All boats in speed championships are equipped with the same kind of motor—it's the shape of the hull and the propeller, and above all the piloting, that makes all the difference.

During one of the first speedboat races on the Seine in Paris in 1880, a motorboat reached the spectacular speed of . . . six miles per hour! At the time, it was a record. Over the course of the twentieth century, technological progress has remarkably improved speedboats. The fastest boats compete in the World Powerboat Championship, dominated by the Class 1 category, which includes catamarans made up of composite material (carbon) that are up to fifty feet in length, and powered by two-thousand-horsepower motors.

Only the most experienced pilots can sail these boats. They sit in the cockpit, which is sometimes covered with a bubble of unbreakable glass. The acceleration is so fast that the boats lift out of the water and the pilots are pinned against the seats. On the dashboard, the speedometer surpasses 125 miles per hour. At this speed, the surface of the water is as hard as the asphalt of a Formula One track!

If you watch an offshore race, you'll notice that the boats rarely touch the water. In order to go faster, the pilots try to avoid the friction of the water, which slows down the boat, by lifting it as far as possible into the air, where there is less resistance. At full speed, only about four inches of the hull remains in the water. Balance is precarious, especially when there is a lot of wind and waves, and, at any moment, if the pilot loses control, the boat might flip over. Piloting demands extreme care and precision.

Using light, high-powered boats, smugglers transport illegal merchandise.

# Famous Boats

The stem of the RMS *Queen Mary 2* (on the left) gives an idea of the impeccable allure of the largest ocean liner in the world. Elegance and authenticity are de rigueur for the *Ranger* (on the right), a sailing boat that made history with its victories in the America's Cup.

Why does a boat become famous? For some, fame came with a specific event, for example . . . a shipwreck. This was the case of the *Titanic*, which sank in 1912. The wreck, found in 1985, has been explored a number of times.

Other boats have become famous because of their incredible size or because they hold records. Currently, the star is the British ocean liner the RMS *Queen Mary 2*, the largest ocean liner ever built. It is 1,130 feet long, 135 feet wide, and 240 feet high, from the keel to the smokestack (the equivalent of a twenty-five-story building). Built in the style of the old transatlantic liners, it can carry 1,250 crew members and three thousand passengers and contains a 1,350-seat dining area, five pools, a spa (which employs fifty people), several theaters, a planetarium, a hospital, and a veterinarian. A real floating city!

Other ships owe their fame to a story or legend in which they play a part. The *Renard*, for example, is known because of the exploits of her captain, Robert Surcouf, a pirate from Saint-Malo who engaged in formidable battles with British trade ships in the Indian Ocean. The *Renard* today is actually a reconstruction of its namesake, which first set sail in 1812.

Finally, some ships have become distinguished in races, like the *Ranger*. This mythic sailing boat, the last J Class boat to compete for the America's Cup in the 1930s, was beaten only one time in practice. When racing, it was invincible.

The *Renard* cruises the open sea.

# Shipbuilders

Until 1970, Europe was the world's leading naval constructor before being passed by Japan and then South Korea. European shipyards today have become specialized, especially in the construction of ocean liners, in order to stay in business. The RMS *Queen Mary 2* was built in the Chantiers de l'Atlantique shipyard in Saint-Nazaire, Brittany.

Night fell several hours ago at the shipyards. But in the midst of all the noise, dust, scrap metal, and paint vapors, workers are laboring around the clock. The bridge of the RMS *Queen Mary 2*, an enormous piece of steel weighing six hundred tons, is lifted through the air by a crane before coming to rest on the ship's deck.

To build a boat, you start by building the hull, either on land or in a dry dock (a large watertight pit drained by pumps). For a wooden boat, construction in a traditional shipyard can take up to several years. A pleasure boat made of plastic can be mass-produced from a mold in several weeks. The hull of a large steel commercial vessel consists of giant blocks made in adjacent workshops, which are then welded together piece by piece with great precision. It's a bit like Legos, but much heavier! For example, for an ocean liner like the RMS *Queen Mary 2*, more than one hundred blocks were put together using more than 930 miles of solder (longer than the distance between Chicago and New York) to make a hull that weighs fifty thousand tons. Using this technique, workers were able to finish the construction of this 1,130-foot ocean liner in just two years, compared with four years for the *France*, a 1,033-foot ocean liner that was completed in 1962.

The largest shipyard in the world is in South Korea. It constructs freighters, oil tankers, and container ships of more than 980 feet in length, at the rate of one ship per week!

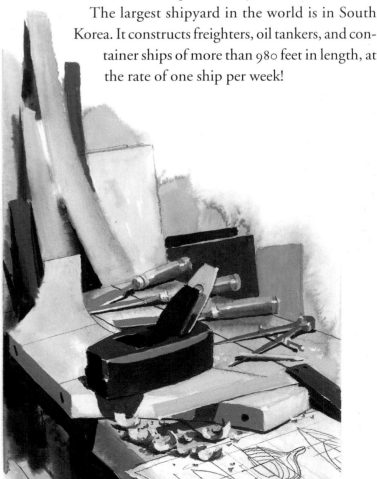

# Ship-breakers

Dozens of wrecks have come to rest in Kerhervy, France, in the muddy estuary of the Blavet River. The oldest among them, tuna boats from the nearby island of Groix, have been beached in this cove since the 1920s.

What happens to a boat that is too old? Sometimes it is scuttled (purposely sunk), but even when run-down and unfit for sailing, a boat can still be valuable: The equipment can be resold, and the material can be recycled. In order to do this, the boat must be brought to a ship-breaking yard.

Some three hundred to six hundred ships per year are demolished in ship-breaking yards, which are mostly located in shallow bays along the coasts of India and Bangladesh. During high tide, a ship is run aground at full speed. Then everything that can be reused is taken apart or cut off. In the developing world, everything is generally carried by hand, including heavy pieces of sheet metal. The labor is difficult and dangerous, but the tens of thousands of workers at these yards often have no other means to support their families.

A problem has arisen. Almost all ships sent to ship-breaking yards today contain toxic pollutants (asbestos, fuel, lead paint), which are dangerous for the laborers and the environment. But most of the demolition yards in Asia are unprepared to deal with such hazardous waste. In order to protect the health of the workers, the boats have to be demolished elsewhere. But the fewer ships that are demolished, the less money the ship-breaking yards make, and many workers have nothing left to live on. What should be done?

**This ship is being taken apart by hand on the beach.**

# Swallowed by the Sea

Run aground on the rocky shore of one of the islands of Aran, in the west of Ireland, this freighter is slowly rusting. Exhausted sailors, an increase in maritime traffic, the failure to adhere to regulations, and outdated ships are the principal causes of most maritime accidents.

If you don't want to end up like this freighter, lifted by the waves and tossed on shore like a toy, a good rule of safety is to always second-guess your position and course, and to recalculate them often. In the sea, you can never be too sure of yourself. The majority of shipwrecks are the result of human errors, and are not due to the material failure of a boat. In the world's oceans, there are approximately two large shipwrecks per week. That makes a lot of wrecks!

After a wreck, the sea begins eating away the ship. Some are thrown up on land, while others disappear completely after several years. Not a single trace remains of the oil tanker *Amoco Cadiz*, which wrecked off the coast of Portsall, in Brittany, in 1978. Because the ship did not sink entirely, the seawater and the salt spray gradually corroded it until there was nothing left. A similar fate surely awaits the rust-covered wreck pictured in this photograph.

The majority of shipwrecks take place along the coast, because currents are stronger and the reefs are dangerous. Shipwrecks are often accidentally discovered by divers, or fishermen who haul up an unusual object in their nets. It must be surprising to catch an antique amphora! Over the centuries, thousands of galleons and warships have sunk in storms or battles. Some shipwrecks hold real treasures hidden in the murky depths of the sea: canons, silver, china, gemstones, ingots, and gold pieces. Dedicated archaeologists spend their lives looking for them—often in vain!

A shipwreck
rests with the fish.

# Ready to Go Sailing?

Whether you are brailing in a sail while balancing on a yard (a horizontal mast), as on the left, or struggling with an immense spinnaker on the *French Kiss*, as on the right, being a sailor is no walk in the park. And in either case, you can't be afraid of heights.

"Pull in the sheet!" "Trim the jib!" Sailing terminology is like a foreign language that all sailors need to speak fluently.

The principal maneuvers on board a ship consist of mooring the boat (attaching it to the quay), casting off (untying it from the quay), and dropping anchor. On a sailing boat, you also have to know how to maneuver the sails. First, hoist them (raise them up), trim (adjust) them correctly to set sail, and then lower them, before folding them up (on older boats, the term is "to brail in").

The sails move according to the "points of sail," which is their position with respect to the wind. Each point corresponds to a sail setting, which can be altered by means of lines known as sheets (which are adjusted with winches). When a boat is close-hauled (sailing upwind), the sails may luff, meaning that they go slack. If this happens, the boat is said to be "in irons." But, little by little, the sails are eased out, until, when the boat is moving roughly perpendicular to the wind (known as "reaching"), they are at their fullest. This is when a sailing boat attains its greatest speed. In order to change direction, the boat needs to go about: You turn the tiller, the sails swing to the other side, and everything must be readjusted. If the wind becomes stronger, it may blow the sails so much that the boat begins to roll over to one side, which is known as "heeling." In order to avoid this, the sails must be reefed, which means the area of the sail is reduced, either by lowering or rolling up a part of it.

So, are you ready to go sailing?

# Navigation on the Open Sea

On the bridge of a ship run by Brittany Ferries, the captain looks at his radar screens in order to navigate the channel that leads out of the port of Portsmouth. Today, electronic equipment and satellite positioning make navigation easier, but they aren't a complete replacement for traditional nautical charts.

Radar screens in the bridge of this freighter display the port's underwater topography. For the captain and the first mate, though, this is not enough to dock safely. They require the help of the local pilot who knows the port like the back of his or her hand. At each port, the bridge welcomes a new pilot on board. To get on and off the boat, the pilot uses a long rope ladder thrown over the hull.

Once a ship leaves a port, the pilot is no longer there to tell them where to go. But as long as the shoreline is in sight, the landscape, lighthouses, and buoys help with orientation. The nautical chart, which indicates the shore, the ports, the beacons, the shipwrecks, the reefs, the depth, and even the nature of the sea floor, is also an indispensable tool.

Of course, when a ship goes offshore for several days, there are no longer any reference points. There is only water stretching as far as the eye can see, and the sun by day and the stars at night. The stars are how ships used to set their course in the past. By using a sextant, an instrument that measures the angle of elevation of the stars above the horizon, sailors could determine a boat's position. But when weather conditions obstructed the sun and the stars from view, it became impossible to navigate.

Today, the sextant still exists (it is even a mandatory piece of a ship's safety equipment), but it is rarely used. Radar indicates the location of surrounding objects at water level, in particular other boats, while a GPS (global positioning system) mechanism calculates the speed and position of the ship to within thirty feet, using data transmitted from satellites orbiting in space.

**The radar and navigation antennae of a French navy escort vessel are vital pieces of equipment.**

# Sea Rescue

Formed in 1967, the National Ocean Rescue Society includes 3,500 volunteer rescuers in 231 stations along the French coast. Each year they help around 10,000 people and 3,000 boats.

The sea is raging, and gusts of wind exceed sixty miles per hour. The Coast Guard launches a lifeboat in these horrifying conditions to respond to a distress call from a pleasure boat.

These lifeboats are present on all U.S. coasts. Once a distress call is received, they only need fifteen minutes and they are ready to cast off. All-weather lifeboats, comfortable in rocky areas or rough seas, respond to distress calls close to the coasts. They also replace helicopters when the wind is blowing too strongly. Towing vessels, like tugs, are required for offshore rescue operations.

Members of the Coast Guard are experienced sailors. The Coast Guard is a branch of the U.S. armed forces and has duties ranging from rescue missions to law enforcement and homeland security. There are more than forty thousand people in the U.S. Coast Guard.

The Coast Guard handles security for the ports and coasts, and runs patrols, allowing the Navy to focus on long-term or long-distance objectives. In addition to lifeboats, the Coast Guard runs a large division of helicopters to help with its missions.

# To Each His Own Port

Set against the backdrop of the Manhattan skyline, the ocean liner terminal lies along the Hudson River, an image reminiscent of the 1930s and the golden age of transatlantic liners. Over the past fifteen years, ocean cruises have become increasingly popular, and the fleet of cruise ships has continued to grow.

Red on portside, green on starboard . . . here we are passing the two beacons that mark the entrance to every port in the world. This ship will soon be moored in a port of call, to take shelter from a storm, or perhaps it's returning home, to its port of registry.

Each port is equipped according to the type of ship that docks there. A marina generally has a restaurant, a yacht club, a sailing supply shop, and sometimes a small work or careening area for making repairs. A fishing port has an auction (for selling fish), refrigerated areas for storing merchandise, and warehouses where trucks load up. An oil terminal has numerous tanks, with a refinery usually nearby. A container port has an expansive storage area and cranes for unloading cargo. Finally, a passenger terminal (for ferries or ocean liners) has a large parking lot, ticket offices, and a boarding area with shops and food stalls where passengers can wait.

Today, some of the world's ports have experienced a rebirth and are expanding thanks to development linked to freighters and cruise ship traffic. Some of these ports have a very long history. The piers that make up New York City's waterfront have hosted transatlantic ocean liners since the mid-nineteenth century, when they left from Europe with millions of immigrants dreaming of a better life in America. Today, tourists on cruise ships are the ones disembarking in Manhattan. They, too, dream of discovery and escape.

**Mobile, modern cranes facilitate the maintenance and repair of pleasure boats.**

# Lightships

Easily spotted with its bright red paint, this lightship topped with a signal beacon is a rare survivor of an era long gone. In fact, there are only about twenty lightships left in the world.

Lighthouses were built to mark dangerous coastlines and to help guide sailors. But what did people do in places where the sea was too deep or the land too sandy to build a real lighthouse? Such conditions required floating lighthouses—otherwise known as lightships.

Lightships were generally painted red to make them more visible. They were held in place by means of anchors attached to two thick chains. The anchor chain might be as long as three hundred feet and weigh up to one hundred tons. Lightships thus remained stationary at sea, an unusual fate for a boat. Sailors on board were continually tossed around by the waves. It was not a job for someone who got seasick easily.

Often, during violent winter storms, a lightship would brake adrift and be carried offshore. Another boat would have to be sent to look for it. This could take a long time, because there weren't even radios on board until 1900, which kept the ships from sending out distress signals.

The world's first lightship was anchored at Nore Sands at the mouth of the Thames in 1732. Today, most lightships are automated, and many were converted to use solar power in the 1990s. Others have been turned into floating museums, restaurants, or even nightclubs.

**This lightship remains permanently moored in place.**

# The Threatening Storm

The Raz de Sein, off the coast of Brittany, is a frothing cauldron where currents flow into the rocky shallows. In spite of the danger caused by breakers, it is a popular spot with professional sea bass fishermen.

This fisherman must be completely mad to be out at sea in such horrible weather! In fact, these dangerous eddies are exactly where he wants to be. He's fishing for Atlantic sea bass, a fish that prefers rough water, because that's where it is easiest to feed on plankton. But if the sea is rough, it is in part because of the dangerous rocks that are only several feet away—at any moment the boat risks smashing against them.

Of course, if you are not going out fishing for sea bass, it is best to stay at home during a storm. No seaworthy sailor neglects to listen to the weather report before casting off. Maritime weather reports are broadcast over the radio and give information on the direction and speed of the wind, the sea conditions, and the regional forecast. This is a fundamental safety precaution.

If, in spite of everything, you find yourself caught in a storm, you should never forget that the greatest danger is to be blown toward land where you might run aground. That's why in stormy weather you should always distance yourself from the coast and take your chances on the open water. Because as paradoxical as it may seem, when you are sailing, the greatest danger comes from the land!

**This ship battles a rough sea.**

# Sailing Schools

Designed in 1948 by the American Clark Mills, the Optimist series remains popular despite having been around for more than half a century. This small beginner's boat uses a type of sail that's rarely seen today: the spritsail.

Learning to sail is more than just learning about the joys of racing in a regatta. In a sailing school, you will learn about the marine environment, the tides, the weather, how to read a nautical chart and understand maritime signal flags, the rules of right-of-way, and sailing terminology. You will also learn how to rig your ship (to prepare it for going out to sea) and maintain it. And, of course, you will also learn how to navigate.

To do this, you need to set sail. The tiller in one hand for steering the boat, the sheet (the line used to adjust the sail) in the other, the novice sailor, wearing a life jacket, takes to the water alone to learn how a small boat reacts to the wind and the waves. You will probably capsize a few times, get the sheets all tangled up, and miss a few maneuvers, but the advice and instructions of the teacher will help you to quickly master the art of sailing.

The little monohull found in many sailing schools is the Optimist. With its flat-bottomed aluminum hull and its single quadrangular sail, it is light, stable, and so easy to maneuver that a child can sail it alone beginning at the age of eight. But the famous Optimist is not only a beginner's boat. In spite of its 7.5-foot length and simple design, the Optimist is also used to sail in regattas. And even on an Optimist, you have to be just as good a helmsman as you are a tactician in order to win.

Most sailing schools also have racing catamarans. The helmsman and the crew hang off the sides of the craft—attached to the mast by a line (known as the "trapeze")—to help balance this particularly fast boat. Suspended above the water like this, you are sure to feel as if you are gliding.

# In the Service of Others

In the frozen Gulf of Bothnia in northern Europe, *Otso*, a powerful Finnish icebreaker, works to clear a route for shipping boats. During the winter months, the economies of Finnish ports depend entirely on icebreakers.

In certain parts of the world, the surface of the ocean freezes solid in winter. No ship can pass through these areas without the help of icebreakers. Their powerful engines enable them to crush thick ice floes without having to worry about damaging the strengthened hull. In this way, they create a narrow path through the ice so that cargo ships can reach their destination.

While icebreakers pave the way for other ships, tugs sometimes have to push them with all their strength. These boats, often appearing minuscule next to the gigantic freighters they help, hide incredibly powerful engines. In ports throughout the world, they help large ships to dock. The maneuver also involves pilot boats, which are responsible for transporting the moorings to the quays. These ropes, as thick as a person's arm, are too heavy to throw onto the quay from a freighter's deck!

Icebreakers, tugs, and even fireboats (equipped with water or foam canons for extinguishing fires) all have names that indicate their use. But what about hopper barges? These barges (flat-bottomed boats without decks) work to keep canals clear of silt. They carry sand excavated by dredges to dump into the open sea.

Offshore, in the wake of Jacques Cousteau's famous vessel, the *Calypso*, scientists are exploring the world's oceans. Some collect information on marine meteorology. Others sound the seafloor continuously in order to provide information for nautical charts compiled by the International Hydrographic Organization.

Even with the diversity of their tasks, all work boats share the same mission: to help others navigate safely.

**This carrier boat can sink itself halfway in order to load up to twenty-five thousand tons of cargo.**

# The *Abeille Bourbon*

Two open-sea tugs keep watch over the English Channel: The *Abeille Bourbon*, based in Brest, secures the area around Ushant, while the *Abeille Liberté,* based in Cherbourg, is responsible for the area offshore of Cotentin. Their rescue operations are generally carried out in rough seas.

In 1978, when the oil tanker *Amoco Cadiz* sank off the coast of Brittany, it caused a massive oil slick. But thankfully the catastrophe at least had one positive result: To keep similar disasters from taking place in the future, the French navy decided to maintain a rescue ship responsible for securing the waters around the island of Ushant in the English Channel.

The area is a dangerous one because of powerful currents, fog, and strong winds. Additionally, there is a lot of traffic: About 150 freighters pass by every day, including a dozen carrying hazardous materials.

For twenty-six years, the tug *Abeille Flandre*, on twenty-four-hour alert, watched over the coasts of Brittany. But as oil tankers and shipping freighters became larger and larger, the French navy eventually decided to replace it in 2005 with a new, more powerful ship, the *Abeille Bourbon.* As a precaution, the *Abeille Bourbon* would set sail from Brest whenever the wind surpassed twenty-five knots, to prevent accidents from taking place on one of the most dangerous and heavily trafficked maritime routes in the world. It has a thirty-five-thousand-horsepower engine to help it reach ships that are distressed (due to engine failures, loss of steering control, leaks or fires) as quickly as possible, and to tow, when necessary, the largest boats in the world, such as aircraft carriers and giant oil tankers. We've come a long way from rescue boats in the beginning of the twentieth century, which were simple lifeboats powered by oars, with no shelter at all for the crew or the survivors! Oars in hand, the rescuers would board distressed ships with only the strength of their arms to help evacuate the crewmembers.

# Belem and *Hydroptère*

From 1896 to 1914, the French three-master *Belem* made more than thirty round-trip voyages from Nantes, its port of registry, to French Guyana and the West Indies. Today, more than one hundred years old, the debonair *Belem* participates in tall-ship festivals across the world.

The year is 1896. The powerful three-master *Belem*, loaded with cocoa beans from Belem, Brazil, is approaching the French coast. The wind and sea conditions are ideal. The crew has taken half an hour to run up the thirteen thousand square feet of sails (they need an hour to put them away), and the ship is traveling at a good speed of eight knots (nine miles per hour). They are preparing to change course by tacking. This maneuver, which requires the twenty-two sails to be readjusted, takes another fifteen minutes, and it could take up to ten hours if there was no wind.

Today, the *Belem*, the sole survivor of the French fleet of commercial sailing ships, serves as a training ship. It welcomes traditional sailing enthusiasts. Sometimes it crosses paths with the *Hydroptère*, a hydrofoil as light as a dragonfly that sails two and a half feet above the water and travels at speeds of up to forty knots (about forty-five miles per hour). For a boat to reach this speed, it is necessary to limit the resistance of the water. The solution? A flying boat, because air offers less resistance than water! Once the windspeed reaches twelve miles per hour, the *Hydroptère's* foils (similar to the wings of a plane) lift it out of the water.

A century of technological progress and thirty-seven miles per hour of speed separate the *Belem* and the *Hydroptère*. And in one hundred years, what will boats look like?

**This hydrofoil uses its own speed to lift itself out of the water, literally flying across the waves.**

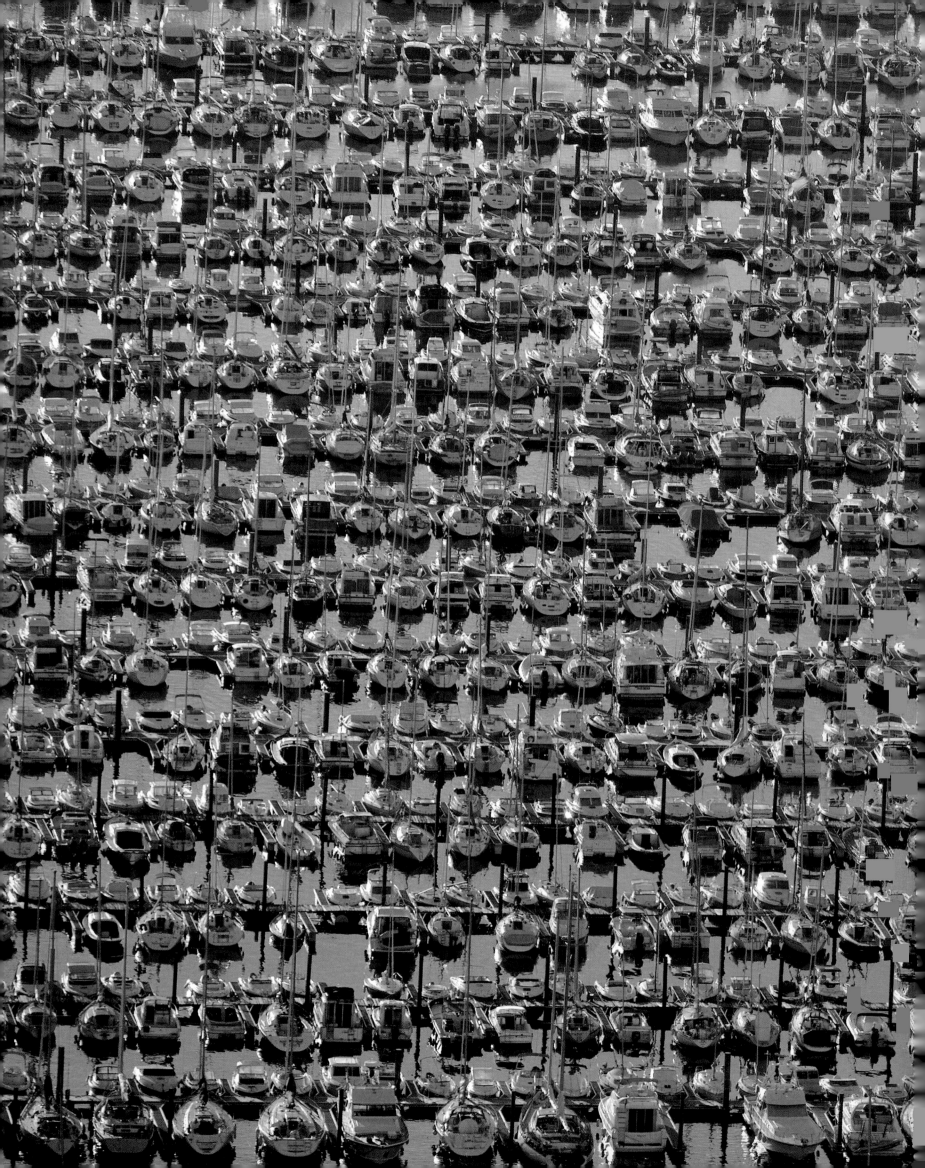